THE MINISTER'S RULE OF DUTY.

A

SERMON

DELIVERED AT THE INSTALLATION

OF

REV. FLAVEL GRISWOLD,

AT SOUTH HADLEY CANAL,

DECEMBER 3, 1828.

BY EDWARD HITCHCOCK,
Professor in Amherst College.

AMHERST:
J. S. AND C. ADAMS,......PRINTERS.
1829.

In the interest of creating a more extensive selection of rare historical book reprints, we have chosen to reproduce this title even though it may possibly have occasional imperfections such as missing and blurred pages, missing text, poor pictures, markings, dark backgrounds and other reproduction issues beyond our control. Because this work is culturally important, we have made it available as a part of our commitment to protecting, preserving and promoting the world's literature. Thank you for your understanding.

Rev. Professor Hitchcock,

Sir—In behalf of the South Society in South Hadley, we tender you our thanks for the excellent discourse delivered by you this day, at the Installation of the Rev. Flavel Griswold, as the minister of this Society—and request a Copy for the Press.

Respectfully, Sir, we are yours,
ENOCH CHAPIN,
WM. BOWDOIN, Jr. } *Committee of*
ELI STEPHENSON, } *said Society*

South-Hadley-Canal, Dec. 3, 1828.

THE MINISTER'S

RULE OF DUTY.

SERMON.

1 THESSALONIANS II. 4.

BUT AS WE WERE ALLOWED OF GOD TO BE PUT IN TRUST WITH THE GOSPEL, EVEN SO WE SPEAK; NOT AS PLEASING MEN, BUT GOD, WHICH TRIETH OUR HEARTS.

It is of high importance that the Christian should possess a fixed standard of duty. Error in the world is so mingled with truth, and sin so often assumes the garb of innocence, or virtue, that we all need some general rule of action—some clew that will conduct us safely through all the mazes of the labyrinth; and enable us to *discern between the holy and the profane—the unclean and the clean:* And the preacher of righteousness stands in peculiar need of such a scale by which to regulate his life: because his deviations and inconsistencies will be more noticed, in proportion as the path which he pursues is more conspicuous. The private Christian, even if a devoted one, may follow in a comparatively retired and unseen course; but the minister of the Gospel is brought forward on a public theatre, where, if he would, he cannot be obscure. He needs, therefore, some immutable principle of guidance, which is applicable in every situation; and which can direct him, as a faithful compass, in the strait-forward course of duty.

Such a principle is given to us in the text. It is the one by which Paul and his devoted associates regulated their steps. IT IS THE WILL OF GOD. In every diversity of situation, among Jews or Greeks, bond or free, learned or ignorant, friends or enemies, the apostles endeavored to speak and act in such a manner as would please God—the God who judged their hearts.

But Paul here speaks of another rule of action, viz. the will of man. He well knew that the desire to please men, and thereby to promote self interest, is the secret spring that keeps nearly all of this world's votaries in motion. He saw this illustrated in the intrigues and flatteries and hypocrisies of courts, and in the forced kindness and attention of the aspiring demagogue. He saw it on the pages of literature, in the fascinations of the romance and the play, in the music of the poem, and in the partialities and unfaithfulness of the history and the biography; and even in the demonstrations of science. He saw it in the time-serving policy of the political turn-coat, in the courage and professed patriotism of the furious warrior, and in the blustering zeal, or dead formality, of the false teacher of religion. In short, wherever he turned his eyes upon this busy world, he saw the ferment of this leaven:—every where, in every rank, the desire to please men was seen to be the secret moving power of human conduct, in spite of every effort to conceal it. But Paul discards such a motive of action with a sort of triumphant abhorrence. It might serve the purpose of the selfish worldling, but not the holy and benevolent purpose of the Christian minister. It demands, however, as the first head of discourse, a few moments examination : and then we shall be better prepared to discuss, in the second place, the superior advantages of making the will of God the sole guide of our actions.

To say in plain terms, that the Christian minister should be entirely guided in his preaching and conduct by a desire to please men, is a statement too gross to be received by any one : and, therefore, it needs no remarks to show the fallacy of such a proposition in its naked form. But the essence of this principle is often urged upon us in another dress, and under a false and deceitful name. The doctrine of expediency often amounts to nothing more than an effort to please men. We consider that a matter of mere expediency, which does not affect any important principle. It was in this sense that Paul said, *all things are lawful for me, but all things are not expedient.* He did not mean that it was lawful for him to commit sin, or to neglect the service of God ; but only, that in regard to things indifferent, such as were in themselves neither sinful nor holy, but only an occasion of sin or holiness, according to the motives with which they were performed ; such as eating certain kinds of meat, and the like ; in regard to such things, he might act as expediency, or policy, would suggest. Suppose now a man regards the doctrines of the bible as of not much importance : he will of course consider it a matter of mere expediency, whether the minister preach them: and therefore, if his people dislike them, such a person would urge him, on the principle of expediency, not to exhibit them ; or to preach them in such an obscure manner, that they would not be displeasing to the unholy heart. Or suppose a man regards church discipline as of little or no consequence : he will, of course, consider it a matter of expediency merely, whether the minister should enforce it. Now the fact is, that very many in the world, who have loose, and inadequate, and merely speculative ideas of religion, do look upon most of its doctrines, and many of its duties, as things almost indifferent: And hence it is, that ministers of the gospel, who regard these doctrines and duties of vast importance, are often censured for not acting according to the wishes of their people, in respect to these doctrines and duties, when they cannot do it, without a sacrifice of principle and a violation of conscience.

But suppose by what is expedient is meant, " not merely that which promotes our present interest and private gratification, but that which is most conducive to the general happiness of ourselves and others for time and for eternity :"* why may not the minister make this kind of expediency the guide of his steps: and surely it ought to please men to promote their best interests. I am willing to admit that such expediency, as this, is a real criterion, or test of virtue ; and could we apply it, no standard of human duty would be better. For it amounts to the same thing as the will of God : since the promotion of the best and

---

* Ed. Encyc. Vol. 13. p. 741.

eternal interests of man is a principal object God has in view in all his dispensations towards this world: so that expediency, in this sense, and the will of God, and the glory of God, all coincide. But an abstract criterion of goodness must be carefully distinguished from a practical rule of duty. The fact is, though God can judge of actions by their tendency, man cannot. Because it is not possible for him—a creature of yesterday, who knows nothing—to calculate the remote and possible consequences of his actions. He may sometimes estimate the immediate effects of his conduct, but he can never determine all its remote effects. True, God has revealed to us the general consequences of virtue and of vice, of holiness and unholiness: But the question we are now considering, is, how shall we determine what is virtue, and what is vice:— what is holiness, and what is unholiness. All will admit, that every action, to be virtuous, or holy, must be agreeable to the Divine Will. But some will say, that the way to determine whether any action be agreeable to the Divine Will, is to enquire what will be its effects upon ourselves and others. And it is indeed true, that in all our conduct, we ought to look at the probable effects of our conduct: and in some cases we may have no other method of determining what is the will of God. But we ought always to remember, that all calculations of this sort upon the final tendency of our actions, are liable to great uncertainty; because we cannot see far enough, nor clear enough, to discern all the remote and possible influence and bearing of our conduct. So that where we have any other mode of ascertaining the will of God, (and in most cases *we have a more sure word of prophecy, to which we shall do well to take heed, as unto a light shining in a dark place;*) we ought to suffer the probable effects of our conduct, to exert over us but a feeble influence. Many a minister of Christ, forgetting, it is to be feared, the example of Paul, and modifying and explaining away the plain commands of God, on account of the dangerous consequences that his imagination painted before him as the effects of complying with their literal meaning, has not merely involved himself in inextricable difficulties, but brought reproach and contempt upon the cause of Christ.

But what, my hearers, would have been the consequence, if the Lord Jesus Christ, if the apostles and martyrs, had acted on this principle of expediency? Christ knew that the effect of his conduct would be, not to send peace on earth, but a sword; that divisions, persecutions and contentions would follow through many centuries; and the apostles found wherever they went preaching the gospel, that bitter divisions and contentions and murders were the consequence of their labors. And what if they had been governed by the doctrine of expediency, and concluded that God could not require of them to do any thing so disastrous in its effects. The result would have been, that no atonement would have been made for our sins, nor the gospel ever have been preached in the world. But these devoted laborers kept in mind the express command of God to go forward; and they obeyed, cheerfully leaving the consequences—portentous as they seemed—to that God who would take care of them and of his cause. And he will guide and guard all the successors of Christ and the apostles, who, in this respect, follow their example.

Look for a moment at the perplexity and inconsistency, in which that minister must be involved, who endeavours to shape his course by expediency: who is more anxious to learn the bearing of his conduct upon the world around him, than he is to ascertain the command of God. In many things, indeed, he might act agreeable to the divine will; since in those fortunate cases in which he calculated aright, expediency would not disagree with the will of God. But in many other cases he would go widely, though sincerely, astray from the path of duty, and dishonor God, and obstruct religion, while he supposed himself laboring for its welfare. For even benevolence itself, however sincere and ardent, will do mischief, unless it receive an impulse in the right direction: and not a few deep and painful wounds have been inflicted on the cause of the Redeemer, by many a worthy minister of that Saviour, because they made the arithmetic of expediency their guide, and neglected the plainly revealed command of Jehovah.

Suppose a minister to be placed among a people who sit uneasy under the plain preaching of the peculiar doctrines of the gospel. He perceives that they are determined not to hear them advocated; and if he persist in maintaining them, divisions and animosities, and probably the destruction of the society, will be the consequence. He becomes alarmed at the prospect before him, and concludes that expediency will justify him in repressing or smoothing over the offensive truths. He does so: and his society remain united and peaceful; and he mistakes the deceitful calm for a token of the divine approbation. Whereas it is in fact a token of abandonment of God: for the union is but the agreement between religion and sin; and the peace but the sleep of death; the prelude of everlasting agony. Souls are not converted: for it is only the truth that makes men free; and where the truth is not preached, they will remain in bondage. And unless the grace of God intervene, the next generation will witness in such a place, a church that has a name to live, while they are dead; and a people ripe for every error and every sin. Had such a minister recollected that his duty was to preach the gospel, that a necessity was laid on him to preach it, and a woe awaited him if he preached it not, God would have taken care of the consequences, and of his cause, and of his minister.

Another preacher's lot is cast where such a laxity prevails in the lives of the professors of godliness, that he perceives the discipline of the gospel must be applied to purge out the leaven. But a violent resistance to his efforts appears, and agitates his church and people to the centre. Shall he proceed, or shall he desist? Expediency answers, relax the rigors of discipline and wait for a more favourable moment: for if you proceed, your usefulness is at an end, and the cause of religion will be injured.—

But the will of God replies: *Know ye not that a little leaven leaveneth the whole lump? Purge out therefore, the old leaven, that ye may be a new lump, as ye are unleavened.*

Again, it may be the misfortune of a minister to be assailed by those who maintain what he conscientiously believes to be deadly error, but who, nevertheless, demand of him that he should cordially receive them to his fellowship, and acknowledge their claims to the christian character. Expediency will whisper in the minister's ear, if you refuse their demand, the cry of persecution will be raised, and multitudes will be led to embrace their errors, who, otherwise, would remain on the side of truth. It will be better, therefore, to yield a little, since less evil will result from this, than from obstinate perseverence, which will look like an exclusive spirit. But the word of God thunders in such a minister's ears, *if there come any unto you and bring not this doctrine, receive him not into your house, neither bid him God speed: For he that biddeth him God speed, is a partaker of his evil deeds. Though we, or an angel from heaven, preach any other gospel unto you, than that which we have preached unto you, let him be accursed.*

Suppose a minister to have no other rule but the will of his people to guide him in his preaching and parochial intercourse; into what a maze of perplexities will he be thrown! One class of his hearers will relish no sermon that is not highly doctrinal, and does not contain the skeleton of systematic theology: Another class demand that nearly all should be practical, keeping the unintelligible mysteries of godliness out of sight. One class are satisfied with nothing that does not make a powerful appeal to the passions, and is not directly calculated to produce strong excitement. Another class can bear nothing that is not measured off and compacted together by the rules of logic. One class look upon it as personal, if the preacher make a searching and pungent appeal to the conscience : Another class are disgusted when he arrays before them, in menacing aspect, the terrors of the Lord. He may find one discription of his people dissatisfied, if all his public performances do nor bear the marks of talent and hard study, and if their minister do not maintain the character of superior genius and scholarship ; and these, of course, would confine him almost incessantly to his study, and leave him no time to go from house to house to learn the state of his people and to testify repentance towards God and faith in the Lord Jesus Christ. But on the other hand, he may find a still more numerous class, who being themselves unaccustomed to the labour of composition, and scarcely realizing that it is necessary for the minister to give himself to reading, in order to maintain his standing and make improvements, have neither any just sense of the time and effort necessary to prepare for the pulpit, nor of the other retired duties of the faithful minister: and these persons, therefore, would demand of him a much greater share of parochial and social visits than is possibly consistent with other duties. This is particularly true in regard to those who have recently entered the ministry. And not unfrequently such an one, in attempting to satisfy his people, has been compelled to steal many an hour from sleep and devote it to study; and thus has the vigor of his constitution been broken down, succeeded by premature decay and an early tomb. Now, if in regard to all these things I have mentioned, the minister should endeavour to make the will of his people his guide, into what a worse than Cretan labyrinth would he plunge! But let him study to show himself approved unto God, and he has only to *preach the word in season and out of season; to reprove, rebuke, and exhort, with all long suffering and doctrine; endeavoring to give to every one a portion in due season; and whether he eat or drink, or whatsoever he do, to do all to the glory of God; then will he prove a workman that needeth not to be ashamed, rightly dividing the word of truth.*

But to dwell no longer on the first part of the subject, I proceed secondly, to suggest some of the peculiar advantages possessed by the preacher, who makes the revealed will of God the guide of his ministrations.

I pause here, however, one moment, to correct a misapprehension, that may possibly exist on this subject. When I picture to you the Christian minister, inflexibly following the will of God in every situation, and remaining unmoved by all the solicitations of man, I fear some will be apt to conceive of such a minister, as a morose, unyielding, monkish tyrant, more fit for the cloister than for society;—better adapted for the dark ages of Popery, than for these enlightened times of Protestant liberty. I fear such is the picture many form in their imaginations, of Paul, and the other apostles, when reading their epistles. But it is an unfortunate caricature : for such steady adherence to the will of God, as a rule of duty, tends to make men like God ; and God is love. It is perfectly consistent with the utmost kindness and tenderness in the minister towards his people ; nay, with a disposition ready to yield in every thing not interfering with duty. What affectionate tenderness is manifested by Paul, only two or three verses succeeding the text, which shows him so resolute in following the will God! *We were gentle among you,* says he, *even as a nurse cherisheth her children. So being affectionately desirous of you, we were willing to have imparted unto you, not the Gospel of God only, but also our own souls; because ye were dear unto us.* And this is precisely the mild and endearing temper, every successor of of Paul, in the holy office, should cherish towards his people.

The first peculiar advantage the minister possesses, whose standard of duty is the revealed will of God, is, that he is compassed about by a bright cloud of witnesses. I will not here point you, my hearers, to that noble army of angels, who 'circle God's throne rejoicing,' and who find in making the will of God their rule of action, an inexhaustible source of happiness. But look at the glorious assembly of prophets, apostles, and martyrs, with the Son of God at their head, and tell me, which of them did not follow, on earth, that same rule, making it the pole star of their conduct? Some of them, indeed, as Moses and Jonah, shrunk, in some instances, from going where God pointed out their path, because it was hedged up with difficulties and dangers: but so far only as they did follow the divine command, were they accepted. And most of them, for their adherence to that command, fell a sacrifice to the rage of man. The Son of God, the chief among ten thousands, the great exemplar of his ministers, made the principle of the text the grand and universal guide of his life. His meat was to do the will of him that sent him: and in the midst of most appalling dangers, he went forward resolutely in the great work for which he came into the world, unseduced by popular applause and uninfluenced by popular hatred. Perhaps no one of Christ's disciples exhibited an inflexible determination to follow the will of God in so many trying situations, as the apostle Paul. The annals of romance and tragedy, do not furnish an instance of more deep and affecting interest, or of greater moral sublimity, than the scene that occurred the last time this apostle went up to Jerusalem. His brethren on the way, forewarned by prophecy of the dangers that awaited him in that city, *besought him earnestly not to go up to Jerusalem. Then Paul answered, what mean ye to weep and to break my heart? For I am ready not to be bound only, but also to die at Jerusalem, for the name of the Lord Jesus.* This same apostle shows how strongly fixed in his mind was the principle of the text, when he says to the Galatians; *Do I now persuade men, or God? or do I seek to please men? for if I yet pleased men, I should not be the servant of Christ.* Recollect too the stedfast resolution of Peter and John, when after imprisonment, they were commanded *not to speak at all, nor to teach in the name of Jesus.* Their reply was, *whether it be right in the sight of God to hearken unto you, more than unto God, judge ye.* A like testimony has been left us in the example of a vast multitude of holy martyrs: And it must be peculiarly cheering and sustaining to the devoted minister of Christ, as he stedfastly presses forward in duty, obedient to the divine will, to reflect that he is treading in the path, which so many distinguished and holy servants of God have marked out, and which they found to be the path to the heavenly city.

A second peculiar advantage of making the revealed will of God the standard of duty, is, that this is always a safe and invariable rule. It is safe for the minister, and safe for the people. Following this, he frees himself from their blood: because he has done all in his power to save them. And if God does not bless his labors to their conversion, he would bless no labours among them. But even in such a case, they do not perish because a false or perverted Gospel was preached to them and they were not faithfully warned, but because they would not be saved. So that however unpleasant may be the faithfulness of a minister, who adheres to the will of God as his guide, there is no danger in it; and if the hearers will conform to the preaching of such a man, they will be infallibly secure. Hence they ought to desire in their minister this faithful adherence to the divine will, even though their sins and danger and folly be set in terrifick array before them: and they should dread, as the severest of curses, a man who cries peace, peace, when there is no peace.

The divine will is also an invariable rule: like the author of the Gospel, it is the same yesterday, to day, and forever. The false teacher, and the man who is permitting a calculation of consequences to guide him, will stand upon one course to day, and upon another tomorrow. The compass of expediency is affected by so many local attractions that it never long remains fixed to any one point. Accordingly, the man who takes it for his guide, must move in a course too devious to be described. Indeed, it is much easier to calculate the orbit of a comet, and as easy to trace the course of the nightly meteor, as to determine the path of him who follows any other standard but God's will, as it is revealed in the scriptures. Be there as much piety in such a man's heart as you please, it cannot save him from great inconsistencies of conduct, so long as he turns aside from the light shed on him by the Sun of righteousness, reflected from scripture, and trusts to the guidance of an *ignis fatuus*.

But the man who follows in the plain direction pointed out by the will of God, moves in a right line towards his object—the salvation of souls and the glory of God—two things always united: and there will be a consistency of character in such a man, that will excite the admiration even of his enemies. Fixing his eye upon the great object of his ministry, and grasping the two edged sword of truth, he advances to the combat, and mows a wide and staight path among God's enemies: And though infidelity, and scepticism, and heresy, and all the hosts that are ranged under the banners of sin, may tremble as they see him coming, and rouse in opposition, and strive to turn him aside from the path of duty, yet when he has passed through their ranks, those who are strewed along his course, on the right and on the left, even when smarting under their wounds, will admire the fortitude and consistency of the soldier of the cross, and some of them will arise, be healed by the great Physician, buckle on the gospel armour and follow him.

A third peculiar advantage of adopting the principle in the text, as a rule of duty, is, that it tends to lead the minister to the diligent study of the scriptures. This is the deep and almost exclusive fountain whence he is to drink in a knowedge of what the will of God is. And although the humblest christian may easily understand the outlines of that system which runs through the bible, yet the most profound scholar needs to devote the labour of a life to fill up all the shades of the picture and give a finishing to the whole. Scarcely a department of science or literature can be named, that does not, directly or indirectly, throw some light on the scriptures. First on the list stands the linguist, with the thread that unravels the entanglements of idiom, and dialect, and usage. Next comes the historian, lifting up the veil of the past, and bringing to light the events and the customs of dark antiquity. Next approaches the metaphysician, to tell us of the various, and subtle schemes of intellectual philosophy, in the Egyptian, the Grecian, and the Roman schools;—whose opinions are sometimes referred to by the sacred writers. And although the astronomer has no material telescope that can penetrate time, as he penetrates space; yet he is able to turn back the keen eye of calculation and examine and establish the scriptural chronology. To throw light upon the same subject, and to point us to mementos of the deluge, the geologist penetrates the earth and brings forth the evidence of former revolutions and the relics of ancient times. The mineralogist too, can throw a brighter splendor upon the Urim and Thummim, and upon the New Jerusalem; while the botanist can make more lovely, the plants and trees and flowers of Judea. Now the more extensively acquainted, with these various branches of knowledge the minister is, the more capable he is of understanding the scriptures. And whatever incites him forward in researches so wide, and yet so interesting, has a happy influence. True, after his deepest search, he will not find specific rules in the bible for regulating his conduct in every given instance: yet he will find general rules, of so comprehensive a character, that if well understood, he need never be long at a loss to know where lies the path of duty. Alas, that so many, who preach the gospel, should prefer directing their people by the result of their own feeble reasonings, rather than bow to receive their instructions from the book of God! It is like following the light of a rush taper, when the sun is shining in meridian splendour.

A fourth peculiar advantage of making the revealed will of God the rule of duty, is, that it tends to make the minister acquainted with his closet. Although he has the bible in his hands, yet he reads there of some who are given up to strong delusions to believe a lie that they might be damned. He finds it there taught, that however clearly revealed are the truths of the bible, and however great the talents of a man, yet he will not see, nor embrace those truths, unless his heart be right. And the wide diversities among men, in the interpretation of the bible, confirms this sentiment. Fearful lest his heart should not be right, and lest he should mistake the will of God, through prejudice and corruption, and wrest the scriptures to his own destruction and the ruin of his hearers, he looks often to that God who can preserve him from error and point out to him the way of truth and duty. Indeed, the chief strength of a minister lies in his closet. He may have talents and eloquence; but if these are not warmed and sanctified by secret communion with God, although he may delight and agitate men, and gain popularity, yet he will not convert them. While the feeblest preacher, whose heart is daily kindled up by a fire from heaven, will see religion flourishing under his ministrations. Let that minister who neglects the duties of secret devotion give over all hopes of success : nay, let him abandon the hope of his own salvation. The Spirit of God will not accompany his efforts unless he pray for it: And if he do not pray for it, it shows that the Spirit of God has abandoned him.

A fifth peculiar advantage of making the will of God the rule of action, is, that it will keep the minister's thoughts habitually directed to the judgment seat of Christ. For at that bar he will be approved just so far as he has acted agreeable to God's will, and condemned just so far as he has neglected it. If this thought be impressed on his mind, it will accompany him in all his ministerial duties. It will give a solemnity and fervency to every private admonition and exhortation, and to every public prayer, sermon, or address. And it is this solemn sincerity, this heartfelt earnestness, which carries conviction to the hearts of men.

A sixth peculiar advantage of making the will of God the minister's sole guide, is, that it furnishes an important defence in temptation. I speak here of certain temptations peculiar to the sacred office ; and these are neither few nor feeble. A man is established, for instance, among a people whom he loves ; and has there laid his plans for spending his days, and provided for the comfortable situation of his family. And besides, if he should be compelled to abandon that situation, he fears he should be cast a houseless wanderer upon the world. But at length he begins to perceive that the faithful preaching of the gospel gives offence, and error is clamorous in its demands upon him to relax his discipline, and be more tolerant in his feelings. In short, he finds that unless he does relax in his faithfulness, he will soon be abandoned and dismissed. Alas, so strong is the temptation to yield to the attack and abandon the ark of God to his enemies, that unless one eye be constantly fixed on the divine commands, and the other on the judgment day; unless he keep up a constant intercourse with heaven, his fears will triumph over his faith, and he will cease to cry aloud, and sinners will cease to be converted. At such a time it is peculiarly important that he look exclusively on the divine will: for if he suffer himself to speculate about expediency, satan will get an advantage of him, and he will inflict a blow on the cause of Christ, which centuries cannot repair. And alike powerful in giving strength to the fainting heart and desponding faith, is this rule of action, under all the temptations to which Christ's ministers are exposed.

Finally, this same principle is peculiarly important in time of difficulty and trial. Were the minister to pass through no severe seasons of this character, he would hardly regard himself a successor of the apostles. But alas, they are planted thick enough along his path, however cheering may be the commencement of his course; and it would be folly to expect an exemption. He is sometimes called to witness his people, in spite of all his efforts, waxing worse and worse; a death like stupor settling upon his church, and sin rioting without fear and without shame among the irreligious. Peculiarly fortunate is it for him at such a period, if he can look back and reflect that his conduct has been directed by the divine will: for then the blood of his people rests upon their own heads; and although he will be pained to see them rush upon destruction, yet will he not fear that he is the cause of their ruin. Times of difficulty and perplexity also sometimes occur in a church, when the fate of the whole body, and of the society in which it is placed, seems to depend upon the course taken by its pastor. Oh let every people, at such a juncture, be delivered from the man, who has nothing surer to guide him, than the uncertain calculations of expediency! But if the revealed will of God be his directory, he need not fear for the church, nor for himself. The faithful minister may likewise be called to feel the deep stabs of ingratitude from some among his people. The more solicitous he is for their salvation, the more are they alienated from him, and imbittered towards him. They hate his doctrines—they hate those duties he inculcates; and throw every bar in their power in the way of his success. Now how shall he act towards such? Let Paul answer: *I will very gladly spend and be spent for you, though the more abundantly I love you, the less I be loved.* Oh, this is an elevated state of Christian feeling: but it ought to be attained by every one set for the defence of the gospel. Yet if a man has regulated his conduct by a desire to please men, how is it possible he should reach this state of feeling towards such! But if the will of God has been his guide, he will look to God for his reward; and can cheerfully go on, laboring for the good of those, who are laboring for his ruin. Thus will he overcome evil with good, and heap coals of fire on the heads of his enemies.

In conclusion of the subject, I remark, first, that the principle, advocated in this discourse, takes away from the faithful minister, a vast load of distressing responsibility. "Duties are ours, events are God's": how much is contained in that sentence! If a man were answerable for all the consequences of faithfully preaching the truth, who would dare ever to preach it! Amid the thousand difficulties that sometimes hedge up the minister's way; under the dark and lowering cloud that sometimes settles on his prospects; borne down by a sense of his own weakness and sinfulness, and beholding the wide wasting mark of sin and error around him, surely he must sink in despair, if he were to judge of his faithfulness, or reward, by his success. But possessed of the consciousness of having firmly adhered to the command of Jehovah, he can go cheerfully forward amid every discouragement: though ten thousand evils cluster around him; come what will come; sheltered under this principle, he knows he is safe, and the church is safe, and heaven is safe.

Secondly. If the minister must make the will of God his sole guide, then how important is it that he keep ever before him, the grand and leading object God has in view in the institution of the ministry; viz. the promotion of his glory in the salvation of sinners! In attaining this most magnificent and glorious object, God has made the minister an instrument: and the grandeur, and sublimity, and unspeakable importance of it, ought to carry him above the low atmosphere of human passions, and make him indifferent to human applause or censure, any farther than these will promote or retard the great work. He professes to be actuated by a higher principle than this world's morality, or this world's philosophy, ever discovered. Let him, therefore, maintain an elevated and consistent course, with the word, and the will, and the judgment of God in his eye. It does not belong to him to descend into the arena of this world's contests; unless it be to bid the combatants no longer to strive with flesh and blood, but henceforth to *wrestle with principalities, and powers, and spiritual wickedness in high places.* It is not for him to employ weapons *that are carnal, but those that are mighty through God, to the pulling down of strong holds.* It is not for him to act upon the juggling and pliable principles of this world's votaries: but the love of Christ should constrain him; and there should be a sort of transparency in his character, that will make it obvious to the world, that the will of God is his guide, and the glory of God his object. Then may he reasonably hope that his labour will not be in vain; and that the souls of those for whom he strives and prays, will become gems in his eternal crown.

May such be your rule of action, my dear brother; such your elevated and consistent course, and such its termination among this people. You know what the will of God is in sending you hither; viz. to labor for their salvation; for *he will have all men to be saved and come to the knowledge of the truth.* This is the grand object you should keep continually before you; and to promote it, may your hands ever be strong and active, your heart warm, and your soul steadfast. Does your heart sink in view of the responsibilities you this day assume? Look up to the everlasting hills whence cometh your help, and remember that you can do all things through Christ strengthening you. Do you fear that your love of souls is weak in comparison with their value? Then turn your eyes, my brother, upon this people, who have chosen you for their spiritual guide. Look at this church, waiting, as I trust, with praying hearts, to be taken by the hand and led into the green pastures and by the still waters of salvation. Look at those descending into the vale of years, and those in the meridian of life, whose hearts have never been warmed by the love of a Saviour; and say, does there not rise within you, a holy ambition, to be the instrument of plucking them as brands out of the burning? Look too upon this rising generation, and see them stretch out to you their hands, and committing themselves to your guidance, tell you, that their eternal destiny depends upon your faithfulness. O, I know your heart burns to make them heirs of glory. And finally, if there be wanting yet a motive to faithfulness, lift up the eye of faith and look to the recompense of reward.

Thirdly. If ministers must make the will of God their guide, then ought their people to listen to the messages they bring, as those who must give an account. It is clearly implied in the text, that if ministers please God, they will not always please men. And such Paul found to be the fact: and so did the Saviour; and so have their faithful successors. It is the minister's buisness to convince men that they are alienated from God, and living in opposition to his laws, and that they must be reconciled to him, or perish. But these are most mortifying truths; aiming a fatal blow at human pride; and it is no wonder that men unacquainted with themselves, should revolt at the painful representation. It is also the minister's duty, sometimes, to show to those who profess godliness, that they *have a name to live, but are dead;* and this, to such, is scarcely more welcome. But let people recollect, when thus excited to complain, that ministers are not to be judged by the maxims of worldly prudence and etiquette. The rule they profess to follow is the will of God, as contained in the word of God. To the word of God, therefore, they appeal: and *if they speak not according to to this word, it is because there is no life in them,* and they are willing to be condemned. But if they go not beyond the sacred record, then should their hearers take heed, both how they hear, and what they hear. *For Christ has said to* ***his faithful ministers, he that heareth you, heareth me; and he that despiseth you, despiseth me; and he that despiseth me, despiseth him that sent me.*** Why do we send for a physician when sick ? That he may exert himself to save our lives and recover our health : nor do we become irritated and offended, because he administers to us unpleasant remedies ; or performs some painful operation, which he declares necessary to our recovery. And why do men settle ministers over them ? That their souls may be saved ; that their spiritual sicknesses may be healed : And yet, when the minister perceives their malady to be too deeply rooted to yield to milder remdies, and finds it necessary to probe their consciences, and to lay open their hearts, by the sword of the Spirit ; how very apt are they to feel as if he were unnecessarily severe, and took delight in distressing them, and in dealing out their condemnation ! They urge the physician of their bodies to let them know the worst of their case : but they would have the physician of their souls heal their wounds slightly, and say, peace, peace, when their is no peace. True, the preacher, if his heart be not right, may mix with the word of God his own spleen and venom ; and thus render the truths of the gospel—offensive enough at the best to the natural heart—still more repulsive. But as I said before, let him be tried by the word of God and by this only. When he endeavours to fix upon the unregenerate man the charge of entire native depravity and enmity to God, let the bible be searched to see if it does not make a similar charge. When he presses the necessity of a renewing of the holy Ghost upon such, and in spite of their depravity, urges upon them their obligations to immediate repentance, let them inquire of Nicodemus whether Christ did not teach the same. When he exhibits the atoning blood and righteousness of Christ, as the sinners only hope for pardon, and justification, let them inquire of the Romans and Galatians, whether Paul did not do likewise. When he insists upon a holy life, as indispensably necessary to accompany faith, let not an antinomian spirit cry out against him, until it is sure the same charge will not lie against Paul and James. When he represents God as having mercy on whom he will have mercy, and hardening whom he will, before he is condemned, let the epistles of the great apostle of the gentiles, be read with prayer. When he represents the future punishment of the wicked to have the same duration as the happiness of the righteous, let them read the 25th chapter of Matthew, and they cannot condemn him. When he exhibits the glorious union of Father, Son, and Spirit, in the Godhead, let them not object, until this great mystery of godliness can be expunged from the bible. And when he holds up the love of the world as a most dangerous idolatry, and makes the most solemn and urgent appeals to every one, to seize upon the passing moment to make his peace with God, let them resolve to comply, or reject the authority of the bible. Finally, let them remember that the day is at hand, when all that the minister has preached will be reviewed : and if he be found to have followed the will of God, every part of his message that was rejected, will hang like a millstone upon the necks of his hearers.

It is these leading doctrines ánd duties, my Christian hearers, which we trust will be woven into the sermons and addresses of the man of your choice, who is now to be set over you in the Lord. These will form the grand starting point of his ministrations : the broad and deep foundation on which he will strive to build up the spiritual house of God in this place. And when we urge him, on this occasion, to keep his eye fixed, in this great work, on the the pleasure of God, and not on the pleasure of man ; when we bid him fearlessly follow the will of God, though it involve the sacrifice of every personal or relative blessing ; though it array this whole people against him ; do we seem to any to undervalue, or treat with negligence, your interests ? Ah my hearers, well do we know that if your minister follow the will of God, your best interests will be infallibly secured. Well do we know, that they could not be promoted by any other course. And from my knowledge of his character, and of this people, may I not predict that a blessed result will attend this union ? Already has God given to you, what I would fain believe to be an earnest of still greater spiritual blessings. May I not hope, may I not predict, that the converting and sanctifying influences of his Spirit, with which he has so abundantly blessed the incipient labours of your pastor elect, will continue to be granted after the ministerial relation is consumated! May I not hope, that this church, impressed with its high obligations to God, and constrained by love to Christ, will, with one heart and soul, continue to compass the altar of the Most High, to plead for still greater blessings upon this place! Is it fancy, or do I see this church in time to come, resolving not to settle down contented with the low standard of ordinary attainments, but to be ever pressing upwards, and setting a bright and most influential example to all around! Do I not see them affording a most prompt and efficient support, by their prayers and self denying efforts, to every exertion of their minister for the salvation of souls! Do I not see this church filled to overflowing, not with those who have a name to live while they are dead; but with humble, firm, warmhearted, enlightened disciples! Do I not see—God grant it may not be false prophecy—do I not see this place distinguished above almost every place, by containing an overwhelming majority of devoted followers of Christ; and showing how happy, how blessed, is a community, which is brought fully under the influence of Christian principles. Should such be the result of this day's solemnities, when you, my hearers, and your minister meet in the eternal world, O what joys,—O what glories, await you there!

Printed by Libri Plureos GmbH in Hamburg, Germany